# Let It Overflow
## Jacqueline James

Let It Overflow
Copyright ©Jacqueline James
November, 2018

*Published By Parables*
November, 2018

All Rights Reserved. No part of this book may be reproduced or utilized in any form or by any means, electronic or mechanical, including photocopying, recording, or by any information storage and retrieval system, without permission in writing from the author.

Unless otherwise specified Scripture quotations are taken from the authorized version of the King James Bible.

Readers should be aware that Internet Web sites offered as citations and/or sources for further information may have been changed or disappeared between the time this was written and when it is read.

Illustration provided by www.unsplash.com

ISBN 978-1-945698-81-1

Printed in the United States of America

# Let It Overflow
## Jacqueline James

PUBLISHED by PARABLES
*Earthly Stories with a Heavenly Meaning*

## Table of Content.

### General

1. Peace — 8
2. Life that Grows — 9
3. The Clinic Visit — 11
4. I Can't Stop — 12
5. Rare — 13
6. Baby Angel Spread Your Wings — 14
7. The Liars — 16
8. Vented — 17
9. Raging Road-rage — 19
10. Every Time — 20

### Spiritual

1. Get Your Holy Ghost Power — 24
2. Jesus Says — 26
3. From God — 27
4. He Lives — 28
5. The Messenger — 30
6. Jesus Wept — 32
7. God is — 33
8. I Believe — 34
9. My Lord — 36
10. Special Weapon — 37

### Educational

1. Parents — 40
2. Your Place — 42
3. Judge Not — 44
4. Senseless Death — 45
5. Tempted — 46
6. Retrain the Parents — 47

## *Informative*

| | |
|---|---|
| 1. Put Some Work In | 50 |
| 2. Life's waste | 52 |
| 3. Father's | 53 |
| 4. Skeletons | 54 |
| 5. The Shooter | 55 |
| 6. Speechless | 57 |
| 7. The Soldiers | 59 |
| 8. When You | 60 |
| 9. Birth Right | 61 |

## *Entertainment*

| | |
|---|---|
| 1. Driving Miss Daisy...Driving me crazy… | 64 |
| 2. Craving | 66 |
| 3. The Piggy Banks | 67 |
| 4. Nature Hair | 68 |
| 5. The Hot Tub | 69 |
| 6. A Hot Day | 70 |
| 7. Dog Sitting | 71 |
| 8. World Pool of Fun | 72 |
| 9. Entertain | 73 |
| 10. All Your Kisses | 75 |
| 11. Slumlord | 76 |
| 12. The Birthday Dinner | 78 |
| 13. If You | 80 |
| 14. Don't Wash My Dishes | 81 |

## *Special Dedication*

| | |
|---|---|
| 1. My Angel | 84 |
| 2. For Your Health | 85 |
| 3. My First | 87 |
| 4. My 'Sister | 88 |
| 5. Sister in Christ | 89 |

## About the Author

  Jacqueline James is a well-known poetess, and the Christian author of the books "Poetry with a Twist," and "The Spiral Affect."
  Jacqueline is on a personal crusade ordained by God Almighty to show the world that God is still in control and His beauty is everlasting. Through her poetry, Jacqueline believes that she is a bridge of communication to inspire, inform, and unite all cultures while amusing them with her crafty style of writing.
  Jacqueline James is an entertainer, as well as a professional writer; therefore, she attends to captivate her audience with a strong positive influence. She intends to mold their characters into acceptance of change, one poem at a time.

## The Dedication

This book is dedicated to my youngest daughter Jeannie Magic Davis. Jeannie has work countless hours with me to help this book become a success. She has given me a vision, as well as an inspiring insight, in-order- to satisfy my readers, with my gift of poetry. She has poured love, and devotion into this book, that allows my audience (you) to have something informative, entertaining, comforting, as well as uplifting within the contents of this book.

Jeannie has helped me compose some of the finest pieces of my work, to be published in this book, to satisfy you with quality material.

Jeannie I sincerely appreciate all your loyally, and patience you've shown throughout this process. Thank you, for helping me make this dream a reality. I love you very much.

## Introduction

    Let it Overflow was uniquely designed into six categories with specific messages to the readers. The general section was made to enhance everyday life situations; while the reader can become inspired by uplifting experiences through the spiritual content. It will present some fundamental values through the educational poetry section. In addition, by reading the informative category, the reader will understand the richness of the similarities of every race of people. The book will keep you laughing and completely amused with the entertainment contents. You will also hear about specific individuals that have left an impression on Jacqueline's life throughout the special dedication section. This book will allow you to explore some of the finest work of poetry, from the very talented author Jacqueline James. It will make you comfortable enough to relax and lose yourself throughout the pages but, find yourself through her poems.

## Jacqueline James

# Let It Overflow

## Chapter 1
### General
1. Peace
2. Life that grows
3. The Clinic Visit
4. I Can't Stop
5. Rare
6. Baby 'Angel' Spread Your Wings
7. The 'Liars'
8. 'Vented'
9. Raging road-rage
10. Every Time.

## Peace...

Peace is a wonderful thing;
It calms you down from every extreme:
It keeps you satisfied with countless measures;
And, it soothes you deeply, with endless pleasures:
Through a storm you will be still;
Because of 'peace,' you're going to chill:
Throughout your life you're going to fight;
But, with a peace of mind, you'll be alright:
Your peace will last throughout your days;
Long as you're willing to humble your ways:
Don't be quick to raise your voice;
Just be quiet, it is your choice:
Be slow to anger, and slow to wrath;
Show the world your better half:
So, just relax and enjoy your day;
You'll have perfect peace in every way:
Joy is rising inside;
Because of peace, I'm very kind.

# Life That Grows...

Beautiful is the trees that grow;
Different sizes and shapes in a row:
Her leaves are brightened from the sun that glows;
Loosely falls as the winds blow:
The oxygen they give is wonderful indeed;
We get as many as we need when we plant their seed:
Populating the land, because they can;
They're created by God and not by man:
Remarkable as they come to play;
Filtering the air throughout the day,
Some green, some small, some tall, some bright;
Sparkling with beauty, from the moonlight:
They feed us all from the North to the South;
We eat their fruits from hand to mouth:
There are extraordinary uses we get from the trees:
Pencils, paper, and honey stored by bees:
From trees we get furniture for all to admire;
From dressers, beds, stools, and closets to hold our attire:
We sit at tables made from the tree stump;
And from trees we get chairs to sit on our rump:
Sometimes we carve our name, and sometimes we climb;
We also sit under them for their shade in the summertime:
Trees protect us all from UV waves;
So, that we can live through brighter days:

They cool the land we live around;
And this also helps keep our energy bill down:
Trees absorb CO2, then release oxygen to breathe clean air;
Which helps to improve our health care:
Trees bring moisture into the atmosphere;
Which saves on water, when they're near:
The protein from the nuts we get from the trees;
Is beneficial to both you, and me:
It's an amazing sight for you to see,
When God created the beautiful tree.

## The Clinic Visit...

I was talking on the phone at the clinic today;
Others all around were picking up on, what I had to say:
As I sat there patiently in the waiting room;
I saw potentials customers, coming my way soon:
They were listening to what I planned to cook;
Which inspired me to write, a recipe book:
I said that I would make some manicotti with cheese;
Stuff with carrots, and broccoli-hold the cauliflower please:
I had my head down slumped over in the chair,
in deep conversation;
But the background chatter blocked my concentration;
So, I set up straight because I wanted to see;
But little did I know; all eyes were on me:
My conversation got humorous, and I began to laugh;
Most of them joined in, at least more than half:
They didn't know what was funny, and it didn't seem to matter;
Because laughter is contagious, and it makes you feel better:
Now, everyone in the room, that I just interrupted,
Didn't want me to leave, but I had to get up!
So, I passed out my cards on the way out the door;
And told them to give me a call, if they wanted to hear more.

## I Can't Stop...

I can't stop writing even if I try;
It's the God in me; I won't deny:
His presence is here in-the-midst of my storm;
I'm cradled safely in his arms:
He wanted me to share with the world a thing or two;
So, everyone will know, what he's able to do:
He lifts me up in my time of need;
And through my faith his love exceeds:
God is my joy in the center of my universe;
He feeds my soul and quince my thirst:
I'm his servant, and for that, I'm blessed;
He humbles my spirit, to give you my best:
Jesus won't stop loving and caring for me;
He won't stop me from writing miracles, so my soul could be free:
It's God's plan for me to achieve;
And, through his grace I will fulfill it I do believe:
His love for me, keeps me inspired;
And, his mercy sets my 'soul' on fire:
I accept his 'will' to be done in my life;
And, I embrace his peace as I go through my fight:
I pray-as-I-praise, throughout my day;
So, my Lord and Savior will have his way:
I'm grateful that my blessings are never blocked;
And I give God the glory, and I will not stop!

## Rare...

I'm obsessed with trying to give the world my best;
Refusing to settle for anything less;
My perfection is what keeps me going;
Knowing true beauty is what I'll be showing:
I have ambition and the will to strive;
The love for my work keeps me alive:
I need to know that you're inspired;
My 'art' is what you truly admire:
When I fill a desire, my 'inner soul' is expressed.
This reassures me that I'm truly blessed:
I'm going through life sharing my charm;
Because I'm at peace in my 'Father's' arms:
I'm very happy that I'm God's heir;
Because he blessed me with a gift so rare:
All this talent is one of a kind;
And, I'm truly blessed, cause the pleasure's mine:
I want the world to see God's light;
Shining through me, from day to night:
Thank you, Jesus, because you care;
I can show the world a gift that's rare.

# Baby Angel Spread Your Wings...

Baby angel spread your wings;
You've gone home to sing for the King
You will be missed, but, you're not needed here;
You're with the master have no fear:

Your job has been assigned to watch over us;
From up in the heavens with God we trust:
You'll sing his praises to start our day;
And watch us faithfully along the way;

We'll worship gracefully until the moon gives her light;
That keeps us peacefully throughout our night;
Now, baby angel spread your wings;
We'll start our day, as you begin to sing;

You'll sing with the love Our Savior brings:
You give us joy throughout our day;
And we'll remember your smile along the way:
Our nights are kept safely, as you stay;
And God's promise is fulfilled as we pray;

## Jacqueline James

Baby angel spread your wings out wide;
So, that we may feel your love, from inside:
You bring us hope in our day;
And, from God's word we will not stray:

Help us to see, the mercy God gives;
So, our souls may be free in order to live:

Baby angel spread your wings;
Now watch you fly;
Watching over us from the sky!

## The Liars...

People who mistreat others are often anxious and self-absorbed
Because of their unkind spirit,
their lies are like a two-headed sword:
They're demeaning and very vicious;
And they spread the 'lies' like wildflowers,
to anyone willing to listen:
It doesn't matter who they hurt, or destroy;
As-long-as they get acceptance through their social core:
They're lacking confidence and have very low self-esteem;
And, they're pathetically insecure, behind the scene:
So, they try to belittle others, because of their own indiscretions;
Nevertheless, they need to know, that life itself will teach lessons:
They'll walk around acting contentious, and bold;
But, sooner, or later, their 'lies,' will unfold:
They'll be left to deal with the mess, that they've caused;
And then, their stability will start to crumble and fall:
Their very reality was built on a lie;
They have no vision in life, and they didn't even try:
These are the people we need to avoid;
Because, if you attempt to get close to them,
they'll make your life hard:
The misery stems deep down in their souls;
And to be perfectly honest, I think it's a black hole:
So, don't be deceived, by their games, or their lies;
Under no circumstances does truth live inside.

## 'Vented'...

We set up for hours talking, me and Shay, my long-lost friend;
She gossips about some things, she'd been holding in,
She talked about the people on her job;
How they've been bothering her for a while:
She said she was tired of them,
and they were getting on her nerves;
But, she refused to tell the supervisor because she was scared:
She didn't want to be labeled as no snitch;
However, she needed that job, so she wasn't going to quit:
So, she pulled them to the side and tried to work things out;
To find out what, all the hassle was about:
When she got an answer, she was really surprised;
They said, they just didn't like her, then they 'rolled' their eyes:
She couldn't believe, they were that immature;
She hadn't done anything to provoke them, and that she was sure:
Now, she was just sitting there in disbelief;
Needing someone to 'vent' to, so she called up me:
She went on to tell me, how they played childish games;
They whispered on their break-time, and even called her names:
I was ' wowed,' and even astound;
Because I didn't think her co-workers
would say "mean' things out loud:
The more I listened, the more frustrated I became;
I couldn't imagine working with someone,
who called me out of my name:

## Let It Overflow

I thought long, and hard, before I gave her my advice;
I didn't want to say the wrong thing,
and changed the course of her life:
I mainly listened, and was a friend to lend an ear;
Because most of that 'stuff' was so harsh, I didn't want to hear:
The only rational advice I could possibly give;
I suggested that she told her co-workers, to live-life-and-let-live!

Jacqueline James

## Raging Road-Rage...

Raging road-rage, throughout the day;
People are driving crazy, and any kind of way,
People will cut you off in traffic, without any notice, or warning;
And put you in a situation that may even harm you:
They don't use their signals or blinkers at all;
But, you will see them on cell phones trying to make a call:
If they keep driving like that, we'll all be in danger;
From the reckless behavior, of a careless stranger:
They'll tailgate you, and blow, and blow;
But you were going the speed limit; you weren't driving slow:
The first chance they get, they pass you up;
And, they "flip you off"-not saying what's up!
Then they'll keep speeding on down the road;
Driving ridiculously, and out of control:
It has to stop, but I have no idea how;
Any suggestions? I need them now.

## Every Time...

Every time that I feel like putting you above anything;
You put me beneath everything:
I sacrifice so much for you;
And for me in return, what do you do?

Many times, you spit in my face;
I'm left feeling like a big disgrace:
"Don't piss on me and tell me it's raining."
Everybody knows, you just be gaming:

I'll give you the world, and whatever's in my reach;
But you don't appreciate it, because you're just a leech:
You're like a maggot, sucking the life out everything you touch;
Regardless of what I do for you, It's never enough:

You're like a cannibal always on the prowl;
Looking to devour your next victim and wondering how:
Every time I give in to you, thinking you're going to change;
You put me beneath your feet, now tell me ain't that deranged?

There's no need for me to complain, or make a fuss;
Cause you just laugh in my face and throw me under the bus:
It's not cool the things you do and the way that you treat me;
What goes around, comes around, just you wait and see:

## Jacqueline James

You always ignore me, and even try to 'dis';
All of your disrespect, I can make a long list:
You had chance after chance to get things right;
Now that I'm fed-up, you want to put up a fight:

Let's keep things real; you were never mine;
Not how you treated me ratchet every time!

# Let It Overflow

# Chapter 2
## Spiritual

1. Get Your Holy Ghost Power
2. Jesus Says
3. From God
4. He Lives
5. The Messenger
6. Jesus Wept
7. God is
8. I Believe
9. My Lord
10. Special Weapon

# Get Your Holy Ghost Power...

I don't understand what's going on with me;
All I know is that my soul is free:
God stepped in and took over my days;
Keeping them peaceful as I pray:
He makes sure my days are bright;
So, I'll be righteous for Jesus' light:
God filled my soul with the Holy Spirit;
And everyone in the church was able to hear it:
The Holy Ghost had his way with me;
He left me with blessings, for the world to see:
I have a gift that was brought, my God;
I'm able to express it when I speak aloud:
Those who doubt, don't understand;
That this was given by God, and not by man:
Everyone wants to know 'Our Father the Creator';
Through the Holy Ghost Power, you won't have to wait for later:
He'll come into your heart if you ask him please;
And stay with you, he'll never leave:
He'll manage your life when things seem to be impossible;
After you have a 'little,' talk with Jesus all things become possible:
I need you to know something about 'Our Father ';
He'll bless you as well, with the Holy Ghost Power!

## Jacqueline James

You must humble yourself to allow him in;
And he'll stick with you, closer than any friend:
You'll be satisfied with what you receive;
When you accept Jesus in your heart and just believe:
Believe Jesus was God's only begotten son;
And he died on the cross, so the battle was won;
Believe he hung alone for several hours;
And rose in three days with the Holy Ghost Power:
If you pray and praise a little louder;
You'll be comforted by the Holy Ghost Power!

## Jesus Says...

Move Satan, get out my way;
My Lord Jesus has the final say:
You may be slick, and quick to move;
But my faith's in Jesus I don't follow your rules:
You think you're smart and know all the game;
I got the power of the Holy Ghost, in Jesus name:
I'm covered under my Jesus blood;
My faith is strong and filled with love;
Victory is mine, and I'm ready to fight;
I'll fight for righteousness to Jesus light:
Now you and your demons just have to cease;
Cause I'm standing strong with my Jesus peace:
My mind is free from your wicked hold;
My Lord and Savior is in control:
I'm not dealing with you, or none of your doubt;
My Jesus laid down his life, in order to bring me out:
God has a perfect plan for me;
He's delivering me from your evil, and setting my soul free:
So, gone satin fine yourself something else to do;
Cause I'm a child of God, and I ain't messing with you.

## From God...

From the richest of the earth,
Two elements of the sea;
The beauty of my Lord is shining through me:
From the top of a mountain, with the roar of a lion;
"Thank You, Jesus"! With my last breath I'm crying:
After all is said, and all is done;
My life was content when I meet his son:
With a million tongues, at a thousand feet:
I'm here to tell you about Jesus' peace:
From the raging river to the battlefield;
You better know that God's love is real:
From the clouds in the sky to the dirt from the earth;
Our souls were saved through Jesus' birth:
From the men that stand to animals that roam the land;
Our Father got this whole world in his hands:
From the trees that grow to the rivers that flow;
Jesus has a plan that we need to know:
Every hour of the day, to the darkness of the night;
God promises to keep us all in his light:
From challenging times to your sickbed;
God gives his word, that's how we're fed:
Like a soaring rocket, to a lightning bolt;
Jesus is always there to give us hope:
From the beginning of time to the end of space;
My life will be complete when I see God's face.

## He Lives...

Jesus was a living sacrifice;
He was crucified on a rugged cross to pay our price;
For the love of all mankind he gave his life:
And we are healed by his stripes:
They beat my Jesus all night long;
For that I sing, with a grateful song:
Mercy and grace, he bestowed unto me;
For my iniquities and sins that he foreseen:
They crowned his head with spiky thorns;
To endure all of our sufferings, Christ was born:
They nailed both of his hands and feet, and pierced him in his side:
He cried out to 'Our Father,' then hung his head and died:
He hung alone for many hours;
To bless us with the 'Holy Ghost Power'
And in three days he rose again with all power in his hands;
To save the souls of every boy, girl, woman, and man:
The blood he shed was for me and you;
To deliver us from all evil, and see us through:
He walked the earth for 40 days healing the sick,
and ministering God's word;
Then he ascended to heaven to be with 'Our Father', to fulfill the
prophecy that was heard:
He was never buried to this day;
He lives through us as we pray:

(Matthew 6:11) "Give us this day our daily bread."
By studying Gods word is how we're fed:
God gave us his only begotten son;
By saving our souls, the victory is won:
No one has never given a greater gift;
As I sing with praise, his spirit lifts:
Love and peace is what Our Savior gives;
And because of our faithfulness, Jesus lives.

## The Messenger...

I did not give them a reason to doubt;
They need to know what I'm really about:
I'm a child of God, and that's for sure; And when I write, my thoughts are pure:
My words are from 'Our Father' above;
He's sending a message full of love:
When you listen closely and hear me out;
You'll learn what faith is all about:
The perfect peace I have within;
Keeps me humble, and without sin:
I want the whole world to see;
How Jesus showed his favor to me:
Through his stripes, I am healed;
Because he died, I can live:
The blood he shed on Calvary;
Was meant to save a wretch like me:
Now, if you want to brag and boast;
Then you need to trust the 'Holy Ghost':
He'll be with you from near to far;
Shining brightly as 'The Northern Star':
If you haven't felt him yet;
Then God Our Father, you haven't met:
His spirit will rage all inside;
Forcing you to swallow your pride:

## JACQUELINE JAMES

All the characteristics you had for a while;
You'll forget them all and become a 'child'!
You need to know, that God's your father;
And you can 'cry out' to him at any hour:
He'll make sure that your days are blessed;
He'll remove the pain, and relieve the stress:
Just put your faith in Jesus, where it needs to be;
Then his love and mercy you'll always see:
He'll be with you to the end of your days;
He'll humble your spirit and change your ways:
I'll know when I'm in my perfect place,
When I see my Lord and Savior's face.

## Jesus Wepts...

We all have our cross to bear;
I'm here to tell you, that Jesus care:
My Jesus' wept, and so will you and I;
Through grace I'm here to testify:
On a rugged cross Jesus was crucified;
He cried out to 'Our Father,' then hung his head and died:
Because of his blood, he shed that day;
God gives us mercy when we pray:
We're not meant to go through life without a fight;
We must fight for righteousness, with humility to see Jesus' light:
When Jesus wept his tears flooded the land;
To save the souls of every boy, girl, woman, and man:
Oh, my Lord, how Jesus did weep;
He put the enemy beneath his feet:
Because of God's love, Jesus wept;
So, all mankind would have salvation left:
I'm blessed because of Jesus tears;
He restored our hope throughout the years:
Because Our Lord and Saviors did weep;
He gave all generation love and peace.

## God is...

Dance in my feet;
Song in my speech:
Love in my heart;
From God's report:
Joy in my soul;
God's in control:
Blood in my veins;
My faith remains:
Peace in my life;
Jesus is my light:
Hope in my day;
Deliverance when I pray:
Healing in my praise;
Help through his grace;
Mercy for my sins;
God's love within.

# *I Believe...*

I believe I believe; I believe it's real;
I would tell you if it wasn't God's love I feel:
Because I believe, peace is mine;
When you look at me, Jesus' love you'll find:
I believe God works miracles, to save a wretch like me;
He delivered me from evil, and set my soul free:
I believe God loves all of us the same;
You must believe as well, and call Jesus name:
I believe God sent his only begotten son;
Because he sacrificed his life, the battle is won:
I believe Our Savior die on that cross;
And pay the price, so our souls aren't lost:
I believe he rose again in three days;
With the Holy Ghost power to change our ways:
I believe he removed the shackles from my feet;
And by faith one day, 'Our Father,' I'll meet:
I believe I'm healed through his stripes;
He died on Calvary to save my life:
I believe Jesus healed the sick and rose the dead;
And because he did, it was a price on his head:
I believe all things are possible through Jesus Christ;
And I believe, he's with me through every struggle and fight:
I believe I'm a better person to this day;
Because of God's mercy, he changed my ways:

I believe God will help you with the things you do;
If you humble yourself, he'll be with you too:
I believe if you come to Jesus and allow him in;
He'll stick closer than any friend:
I believe he'll do the same for you as he's done for me:
He'll carry your burdens and set your soul free.

## My Lord...

My Lord is going to open up the windows of heaven and pour me
out an abundance of blessings,
And I won't have room enough to hold them;
And a thousand tongues wouldn't be enough to thank him:
My cup will run over with all of God's love, mercy, and grace;
My life will be filled with peace,
and joy until I reach that Holy place:
My blessings will come in all good health;
My blessings will come to increase my wealth:
He'll keep me in his perfect peace;
My faith in Jesus will only increase
My Lord will make my worries go away;
When I spend my day with him and pray:
He'll be my shelter in a storm;
My Lord is where my strength comes from:
And I have all these and more reasons;
To thank you, Jesus.

## Special Weapon...

The Holy Ghost has a special power;
It's there to protect you at any hour:
When you want a special weapon, to use the most;
Then you better call on Jesus for the Holy Ghost:

It'll protect you from your enemies, with its special shield;
And bless you with a righteous life to live:
It'll get inside of you, and be real bold:
The next thing you'll know it's God in control:

The Holy Ghost will fight your battles in your time of distress;
And the whole world will see that you're truly blessed:
The Holy Spirit has a perfect plan that's right for you;
'Peace be still' and let God's love shine through:

The Holy Ghost is your special weapon;
It's always there, regardless of what's happening:
The battle you're fighting is already won;
When you were blessed with the Holy Ghost through Gods son:

It'll move you where you need to be;
And Gods light will shine through you, for the world to see:
You'll speak in tongues, along with other saints the same;
When you all pray together in Jesus' name;
*Continued On Next Page*

# Let It Overflow

We all need the Holy Ghost power;
Only through Jesus can we reach Our Father!
God hears us when we speak in a Holy tongue;
And this wards off demons when we talk through his Son:

Pentecost is a blessing, with all the saints on one accord;
God shows his mercy when we cry to Our Lord:
Miracles, healing, and deliverance take place
during the Pentecost days;
Through our special weapon the 'Holy Ghost,' our souls are saved!

## Chapter 3
### Educational
1. Parents
2. Your Place
3. Judge Not
4. Senseless Death
5. Tempted
6. Retrain the Parents

## *Parents...*

Our parents are here to console, and love us along the way;
They usually do their best for us, to have an amazing day:
They plan our days to make them comfortable and easy;
But, when we don't follow their schedules, it's not very pleasing:

After, we go against the rules, and end up caught;
Then, we try to argue, that we have our own thoughts:
They spend their time guiding us, and ordering us around;
By the time we decide to listen we're fully grown:

They tried to stop us gently from making any mistakes;
And we don't realize until later the advice they gave was great:
They get on our nerves and aggravate us
But, we constantly rebel, and put up a fuss

Nevertheless, they put up their best efforts to keep us in line;
And, we follow a few rules to gives them peace of mind:
We're older, but not grown, so we don't get an opinion;
Our voice is only heard, to agree with their decision:

By the time we get old enough to talk to them,
they don't understand;
So, trying to make sense of things,
I hope wasn't in your plan:

JACQUELINE JAMES

Half the time they don't know
if their coming are going,
they don't comprehend;
So, it's best to let them have their way, and try to be their friend:
Now, the 'role' has reversed its self,
and we're here to love them
and give them care;
And we must watch them faithfully,
cause they're the reason why we're here.

## Your Place...

We all have a role to play;
Good or bad at the end of the day:
Rather sane or not, or just an illusion;
Nevertheless, we draw our own conclusion:
It's a place in this world for all of us;
We pray for a proper fit, 'In God we trust'!
It's a need for us all, to know our place;
To avoid embarrassment, or losing face:
It's frustrating when we don't know our actual call;
We start to resistant, and build up a wall:
We often wonder who we're meant to be;
We must get to know ourselves to reach our destiny:
Sometimes our purpose is not always clear;
We have things to get pass, to overcome our fear:
We spend our time searching on a mission;
To get our point across, and make sure the worlds listens:
You must understand, to know your place;
There'll be difficult times, and challenges to face:
You might be a banker or a lawyer;
A housekeeper or a gardener:
A sister, a brother, a wife, or a mother;
Or maybe a firefighter, or the police,
A counselor, a cook or even a priest:
You might become a doctor or even a speaker;
Or maybe an athlete who like to wear sneakers:

What if you're a plumber or a teacher;
Or you might be filled with the gospel and become a preacher:
You might become an uncle, a daddy, or a friend;
Or end up being a mad scientist who doesn't comprehend:
You can become a janitor, a coach, or a nurse;
Or maybe you only can fix the straps on a purse:
You might give world-wide discussions;
Or work on the streets, during construction:
You might be a musician who plays in a band all day long;
Or you might become a vocalist who sings a great song:
You might be a dancer, or you might work on a farm:
Or maybe a bodyguard who always stays armed:
Maybe you're baker, or an electrician;
Or you might become a politician, with an important position;
Or maybe a mailman, who's forced to use mace;
Perhaps you're a ballet dancer full of grace:
You might become a painter, a cashier or a writer;
Or a court judge that makes everyone's load lighter:
Maybe you're just confused and have lots of issues;
Or you're just a big crybaby, who needs plenty of tissue:
Whatever it takes to put a smile on your face;
You'll be truly content when you find your place.

## *Judge not...*

Short, gay, black, fat, or white;
Just remember God made you right:
Young, thin, straight, or old;
We all bear a spiritual soul:
Tall, thick, tiny, or brown;
You're also worthy to wear a crown:
Homeless, famous, starved, or rich;
You'll show humility if you had to switch:
Little, average, brilliant, or slow,
You're just as important, and you need to know:
Hideous, commons, pillars or greeters;
They're all capable of being a leader;
"Those without sin, cast the first stone."
If you know a person without flaws, then you're on your own:
We all have things in our lives to overcome;
We can be strong, and face them, or weak and run:
Whatever the situation might involve;
We do whatever it takes to fix or solve;
While you're pointing your finger at me to blame;
Your thumb's pointing back at you, just the same:
Now you're quick to judge but slow to admit;
We all have issues that we need to quit:
So, judge not, or be judged in the end;
And, I promise my friend, you're not free from sin.

## Senseless Death...

Senseless deaths, way too many,
Gone too soon, for no reason if any;
Taking from this earth without a clause;
They didn't hesitate; they didn't pause:
Your life can be 'zapped' any minute of the day;
To them, it doesn't matter, and it's not okay:
The evil is progressing, and becoming strong;
And killings are treacherous and very wrong:
We're all affected one way or another;
And, it hits hard when it's our sister or brother:
What's it going to take to make them stop;
Sometimes the killings are from our cops:
These people are possessed by evil to kill;
They're without 'joy,' or reason to live;
Their hearts are empty as a black-hole;
They're without Jesus to save their souls:
It's happening so often, and over again:
They'll kill your mother, children, or friend:
There's no escaping; there's nothing you can do;
And, you don't get a warning if they come to kill you:
So, my only advice to keep you safe;
Pray to Our Father, for his mercy and grace.

## Tempted...

Temptations are something so powerful, and strong;
Then, you're left singing the same old song:
Old habits are hard to break;
Especially when you're making the same mistakes:
It may not be good for you, but when it feels good to you:
You continue to do, the things you do:
Disregarding the ones close to you;
And, sometimes neglecting responsibilities too:
We're often tempted by the things we're around;
A smell, a touch, or even a sound:
It makes us want to explore 'that' thought:
And, return to the same thing God brought us out:
But, I'm here to say, just stay strong;
Keep your faith in Jesus; you're not alone:
Cause if you return, there are consequences to face;
You acquire seven more demons if you fall from God's grace:
God is forgiving, and you can repent;
His mercy endures forever, that's why his son was sent:
We've all been tempted, and we've all fallen short;
But, we're given more than a second chance,
with Jesus in our heart.

# Retrain the Parents...

Retrain the parents, so they'll understand their role;
As the parents, they're obligated to take control:
All the children are running wild;
They must be reminded they're just a child:

Give them something age appropriate to do;
Then, they won't end up disappointing you:
Stop, trying to be their friend;
And allowing the foolishness to come in:

Give them love and support in your home;
So, that they won't end up, on the streets alone:
Parents, don't go out to 'party,' with your children;
If you do, it's sure to ruin them:

Educate your children from the womb;
They'll have life challenges to face soon:
Children mimic all things, that's new:
Be mindful of the things that you expose them too:

The stuff they see you do, they will mock;
So, if you're doing something inappropriate, please stop:
People, please don't have children for the appearance;
When you're lacking parental skills and experience:
*Continued On Next Page*

## Let It Overflow

You must be willing to make a full commitment;
So, your children don't grow up with hatred, and resentment;
Parents, listen up and pay attention;
Your children need spiritual guidance and a lot of discipline:

God created the man and woman to reproduce;
To replenish the Earth and enhance its use:
So, before you make the decision to become a parent;
Please make sure that you understand the 'title',
and you've learned it.

## Chapter 4
### *Informative*
1. Put Some Work In
2. Life's waste
3. Father's
4. Skeletons
5. The Shooter
6. Speechless
7. The Soldiers
8. When You
9. Birth Right

# Put Some Work In...

I'm trying to get some work in;
Between two girlfriends, a part-time boyfriend,
and a long-distance sister friend;
And I'm just trying desperately to put some work in:
My sister-friend lives out of state, but she 'skypes,'
me during the day;
We like to laugh, and joke about our lives,
that's the only way we get to play:
In the evening, I get calls from both my girlfriend's;
They want me to hang out, but I must put some work in:
Is hard for me to think clearly and write;
Because every night my boyfriend likes to argue and fight:
My work is what I prefer to do;
And I hope you know; it's not bothering you:
When I'm writing, I'm feeling great;
I write in the morning, and I stay up late
I'll stay up through the entire night;
Working until the morning light:
I don't have much of a social life;
But, as-long-as I'm working, I'm feeling alright:
I can't stop it, even if I try;
I dream of writing; I can't deny:
Support my work; I wish you would;
My writing comes; first, I thought you understood:

## JACQUELINE JAMES

I'll take a break every now and then;
And, hang out with my family on the weekend:
I called my boyfriend on the phone;
And tell him he's welcome, to come along;
My girlfriends know they're welcome, as well;
So, I invite them too, so they don't yell;
We all have a really, good time;
And, I write about the memories, cause they're mine:
Writing is my entire life;
It keeps my days full, and bright:
So, if you want to stay my friend;
Just accept it when I put some work in!

## Life's Waste...

I didn't put it there, so I'm not going to pick it up;
It's not my business, so why should I care about the 'smut':
Sometimes "life's waste" lands right in our front yard;
To look away, or ignore it, will be hard:
God kept me safe while I slept;
But when I woke up, trouble fell in my lap:
Am I not, "My Brother's Keeper'?
I don't get that right to deny God's people?
Through God's word, I'll make a connection;
And, his blood, will bring about, the protection:
I don't scrutinize, nor do I judge;
Jesus died to forgive, and bring Our Father's love:
My place is here to do my Father's will;
And, to understand, that our Savior, died so that we may live:
I don't have the right, to deny my brothers of anything;
Because they're also here to meet The King:
God deals with what we call "life's waste";
Some of us go through hardship,
and we're redeemed through God's grace:
He gives us all the choice, to be born again;
Regardless, of our iniquities and our sins:
So be caution, before you refuse, or deny "life's waste";
Without God's grace, you would've been in their same place.

# Father's...

Fathers are born to conquer the world and some;
They take care of their families as they come:
God put them here to be strong and wise;
And to take care of the children of every size:
He knows his role and his obligations;
And he carries it out with great dedication:
He helps his family to understand;
That God is the reason for his plan;
We often rely on our father to come through;
When we're not quite sure of what to do;
He helps to guide us in the right direction;
And he does it all, with great perfection:
Fathers are there when you're least expected;
They keep us safe, and well protected:
His role is serious and sometimes complicated;
Nevertheless, he fulfills it, and its stipulations;
He's a hard worker made in God's image;
And he was born to procreate so the world may have plenty:
And we're all truly blessed to have fathers to lead us,
and guide us along the way;
And may God bless you'll on this Father's Day!

## Skeletons...

Skeletons in our closets;"
Things we do, when life allows it:
Secrets from our past;
The truth will soon surpass:
You can't get away from the things you do or say;
They'll eventually catch up with you one day;
Your skeletons will come out, and be here to stay;
And, you'll be left with the repercussions to pay:
Now, you're embarrassed by the things you used to do;
However, what you've done in your past,
doesn't necessarily define you:
You try to escape from your past, and forget;
But, it's very much necessary to repent:
Your "skeletons in your closet," don't just fade away;
The may just surface to 'haunt' you one day:
Your 'skeletons' don't just affect you alone;
They affect others as well, even after the time is gone:
So, be cautious of your actions from the start;
Then future 'torments you will avoid:
We all have a past, that will eventually surface;
However, if there are "skeletons' from our closet,"
it won't be nice, and that's for certain.

## The Shooter...

A man got shot, his name was 'B';
It was witnessed by a man fixing the electricity:
He was a neighborhood friend of a friend-of-mine;
She quoted that his spirit was very kind:
'B's lady came outside to see what was the matter;
The shooter, shot her as well, and her blood then spattered:
The shooter got in his car and drove away;
And, he took another life before the end of the day:
The man's life he took name was D;
And he was the husband of a lady that's special to me:
The shooter then drove away to a nearby state;
He was found by the police the next morning late:
He was found walking down the highway, stripped of his clothes;
Murmuring something evil, nobody knows:
I found out later in conversation;
That the shooter was a friend of someone related:
They said that he was a nice person,
who wasn't like that in the fall;
And, that they couldn't understand how he killed them all:
They didn't believe that he could be so cold;
Then, I just replied, that the devil stole his soul:
These events turned our community upside down;
But, we all were relieved when the shooter was found:
Continued On Next Page

## LET IT OVERFLOW

We all want justice for our loved ones;
And, we all want to know why he killed everyone:
Society will lock him up, and study his brain;
And, try to determine why he went insane:
But, God already answered me;
The shooter was possessed by evil, and his soul wasn't free.

## Speechless...

A long time ago I didn't want to speak;
Someone snatched my innocence, and made me weak:
But before that day, I learned how to walk;
The first thing I learned was how to talk:

I spoke simple words, and they were clear;
The ones who heard them were blessed to hear:
My mother often bragged on, the knowledge I had;
A lot of adults gathered around to listen, and they were glad:

My words were uplifting, even as a child;
And the ones who heard them were inspired for a while:
They would return to hear more, and gave me money;
And at the time, I was a 'child'...and thought it was funny:

Something happened and blocked my thoughts;
It left me speechless without a doubt;
My voice wasn't heard for years to come;
My innocence was snatched, and it wasn't fun:

It wasn't my fault, 'so they say';
So, why did I live such lonely days?
Yeah, I went on to prosper, and had some good times;
But I was never able to express my rhymes:
*Continued On Next Page*

# Let It Overflow

But now I'm back, strong as ever;
'Spitting' real hard, it's now- or- never
I'm 'spitting' hard, and I'm 'spitting' fast!
Whatever I'm 'spitting' it's meant to last!

When I 'rap,' I got lots to say;
If you ain't down with me, get out my way!

## The Soldiers...

For all the fallen soldiers
who fought for this country with their lives;
Some of them left behind
mothers, fathers, sisters, brothers, and even wives:
May God bless them all for their courageous acts:
Their sacrifices have made our lives more tolerable,
and that's a proven fact:
Unfortunately, blood was shed, and lives were lost;
However, when you at war, you must pay a cost
All our soldiers were honorable and brave;
Because of their fight, our 'way' was paved:
Thanking them today will never be enough;
Some things they endured were unspeakable and tough:
Nevertheless, we thank you for granting us a better life;
To be able to live more feasible after your sacrifice:
When we look at a soldier we can always find;
A truly brave hero of 'his' time:
Thank you, Jesus, for the soldiers who relentlessly fought;
They left their homes to fight
for our country, without a second thought:
Each of them knew that they might never return;
Nevertheless, they went to war, and their metals all were earned:
We appreciate all their efforts, and yes, we're very proud;
That's the reason we celebrate Memorial's Day
and called their names out loud.

## When You...

When you give up your turn, for an older adult, then that's fine;
And, when it's done without haste or complaint, then that's kind:
When you do what you're capable of, then that's good;
But, when it's done to the best of your ability, then you should:
When you give someone your last, then that's nice;
And when It's done more than once, it's a sacrifice:
When you greet people politely, then that's right;
When you're humble, instead of harsh, there's no fight:
When you treat others with chivalry, then that's respect;
When you need a favor returned, they don't reject:
When you love those who hate you, then that's obedience;
When they continue to hate and mock you, then that's their deviance:
When you laugh, to keep from crying, then that's good will;
And when no weapons form against you, then that's God's shield:
When you're slow to anger, and wrath, then that's humility;
And when you show meek, and kindness then that's serenity:
When you show your strength through courage, then that's power;
And when you give God the glory, then that's honor:
When you're quiet through your storm, then that's faith;
And when you're blessed because of it, then that's grace.

# Birth Right...

You have no idea the struggles that I had to overcome;
I made it through with grace, and Jesus' love:
My story is my own quest through life;
I earned the right to see Jesus' light:
My faith brought me to where I am;
If it weren't for mercy, my soul would be damned:
All the things that I went through;
Was a testimony to share with you:
From all the stuff in my past, I should've been dead;
But I know now, that it was just satin trying to get in my head:
He'll stick around if he thinks you're weak;
To make sure you're vulnerable and willing to sink:
He'll try to cause you pain and make you hurt;
But I'm here to tell you, that his tricks don't work:
There'll always be some challenges to face;
However, victory is waiting through Jesus' grace:
Make no mistake; I'm no different than you;
I had to bow down, and become humble too:
I had to pray for deliverance, to remove the shackles from my feet;
In order to become righteous for Our Father to meet:
God is my all and all;
In the midst of my storm, I can always call:
*Continued On Next Page*

## Let It Overflow

I can count the blessings Our Father gives;
My cup runneth over because Jesus lives:

"Lord all of the things that I had to go through;
Were just a test to get closer to you"
God gives us all the same choices in life:
To accept Jesus as our savior, it's our birthright.

## Chapter 5

### Entertainment

1. Driving 'Miss Daisy'...Driving me crazy
2. Craving
3. The Piggy Banks
4. Nature Hair
5. The Hot Tub
6. A Hot Day
7. Dog Sitting
8. World Pool of Fun
9. Entertain
10. All Your Kisses
11. Slumlord
12. The Birthday Dinner
13. If You
14. Don't Wash my Dishes

## Driving 'Miss Daisy'...
## Driving Me Crazy...

It was four different doctors my mother went too;
Just to acquire different bills, when she was through:
She missed the last step at her house;
That's what all this nonsense, was about:
Her foot was swollen, and it was sore;
But, she went on in the house, and slammed the door:
I asked her nicely, to go get it checked out;
But she refused to listen, and began to 'pout':
She soaked it in some green alcohol;
She, rubbed it gently, and that was all:
Then she wrapped it up neatly and put on a house shoe;
And continue to do, what-she-do!
She went up and down the steps as if she was well;
But, as she walked about, it continued to swell:
Two weeks later, she called my phone;
And, said, "baby I think we need to go to the doctor, after all"!
It was very late in the afternoon;
But, I got up, got dressed, and took her to the emergency room:
They took an x-ray and told her it was broke;
And, told her finger was broken as well, and that's no joke:
They had to cut her ring off her finger, but she didn't put up a fight;
As-long-as when she left, she would be alright;

## JACQUELINE JAMES

They put her foot in a walking boot;
And, she pranced around, and looked real-cute:
They told her that she couldn't drive;
Other than that, she'd be just fine:
They gave her some pain pills and sent her home;
And, told her to follow up with her doctor, but don't wait too long:
She called them on the telephone;
And, I had to drive her, so I came along;
They sent her to someone who specialized in broken bones;
And, it was a long way, from her home:
I drove her to the specialist, that was far from her house;
I drove around for an hour, and I got lost:
When we finally arrived, it was a relief;
But, when the doctor saw how well she walked,
he was in disbelief:
They put her foot in a bigger 'boot';
And, told her to get rid of the old one, and wear the new:
But, they said her finger was not their expertise;
And, she needed to go to a different specialist to meet her needs:
So, they gave a referral to call on the phone;
To a different specialist when she got home:
I drove her on the appointment day;
And, she was laughing the entire way:
They told her that she could go to therapy;
Or, just soak her finger if she was worried:
The day had come for her follow-up;
And she walked so fast; I could barely keep up:
I drove her there, cause I was pleased;
And, the doctor removed the boot, with lots of ease:
They told her that, she could drive again;
And, that news was just a win-win:
Cause, I was driving her around for a month,
like she was 'Ms. Daisy';
And, "believe me-you," she was driving-me-crazy!

## Craving...

The salt, the meat, the sweet, and the treats;
They're all good when you need to eat:
Craving peanuts, popcorn, and pretzels, all salted to your taste;
And, you licked the bag, to-be-no waste:
All the things you like to munch;
Are very loud, with a great big crunch:
Eating turkey, chicken, roast, and steak;
Served with two sides, don't make it late:
Muffins, cookies, cakes, and pies;
Set on a platter, before your eyes:
Now, you know you want them, sweets;
But, you can't have any, before you eat:
Taffy, caramel, chocolate candy;
You keep them close, and keep them handy:
They're everything you like to eat;
But, you know you got those cavities:
You crave them more, and more each day;
You'd eat them all if you had your way.

# Jacqueline James

## The Piggy Banks...

The piggy banks from my past;
They held a mini fortune of cash:
I cracked them open to count that 'dough';
It was lots of money, little did I know:
Over the years, I had been saving up;
And after I counted, it was over a few thousand bucks:
So, I ran to the bank to cash it in;
And, when I got back home, everybody wanted to be my friend;
They wanted to go out, and party at my expense;
But I said "Y'all know I got bills, and I got my rent":
So, they all sat around, and I was wondering why;
They were just waiting to see, what I was going to buy:
I wanted some new clothes, and I needed some new shoes;
But, I wanted to go on a weekend getaway, and break the rules;
As I sat back thinking, trying to decide;
My cousin stopped by, selling a real nice ride:
Now I'm all over it, because I like that car;
But if I bought it, my money wouldn't go that far:
So, I went into the house just to ponder a little longer;
I was trying to come up with a purchase, that'll make me stronger:
Now, what could I possibly spend all this money on?
That will make my life happier when I got back home:
So, I thought, and I thought, and I thought again;
Then, it finally hit me, how much I was going to spend:
I bought one big piggy bank, and I put the rest in!

## Natural Hair...

Curly, straight, puffy, and braided;
It's not permed, but it's wavy:
It's the way that we style our hair;
Just, keep it natural if you care:
You were born to be unique;
So, embrace your style and your technique:
Let your hair down, or braid it up;
Or puff it out, and wear it rough:
Crinkle it, or press it out;
Show the world, what it's about;
Give yourself, what's owed to you;
Comb your hair, and make it-do-what-it-do:
Or, shave it off, and wear your skin;
And, show your natural-beauty, within:
You can wear a wig, or wear the weave;
But, your hair's still there, I do believe:
Be about the natural stuff;
Wear the dreads, or afro-puffs:
You're looking good when you're natural;
See, all the beauty, you have captured!

## The Hot Tub...

I'm in the water, I'm half-dressed;
The bubbles are soothing, relieving stress:
I'm in a hot tub, there are others as well;
But I'm in my own 'world', so I couldn't hardly tell:
The water's hot, but that's okay;
It helps me to relax, in its own way:
My bones were aching, from my neck to my crack;
But, the bubbles are relieving the pain through my back:
After I sit in the water 30 minutes, or more;
I suddenly realize, I'm no longer sore:
I was laying there peaceful, looking up at the ceiling;
I could hardly believe; how good I was feeling:
It took my pain; sent it soaring away;
And, that made me have a more wonderful day:
And in the future, I won't need a back rub;
Because, all I'll do, is sit in the hot tub:
I'll be back when the pain comes again;
Because it was so satisfying and fulfilling within!

## A Hot Day...

I went to the park to have me some fun;
To, listen to the music, and get me some sun:
I played with the children, then we sat down and ate;
I came back home when it started to get late:
My body was so tired, as I came up the steps;
I wobble up each one, moving from the right to the left:
I made it to the top, and into the house;
I had a real good time, but my body paid the cost:
I came into my room and flopped down on the bed;
And in three minutes, my blood rush to my head:
I was trying to make it from my bed to the tub;
Cause, I was sweating, and smelled like an outdoor 'thug':
I finally got up and start moving around;
I took two steps forward, and fell back down:
But, I needed some water on me, so I pushed real hard;
I made it to the bathroom, and fell into the tub forward:
I washed and scrubbed until my skin came clean;
Then, I crawled out slowly, so I didn't make a scene:
I got in my bed, all cleaned up, and feeling good;
And I went to sleep instantly; like I knew I would.

## Dog Sitting...

My daughter went on vacation and left me in charge to dog-sit;
She had a spoiled Shih Tzu and a playful Pit:
Every time I sat down the Shih Tzu jumped in my lap
for me to rub him, and never stop;
Then along came the Pit, and tried to block:
The Pit walked around all day with this squeaky ball in her mouth;
It was her favorite toy, and she refused to spit it out:
As I sat on the couch rubbing the Shih Tzu comfortably;
The Pit walked by, and had to bother me:
I had one arm swinging from my side,
while I was sitting on the couch;
And, here she comes with this squeaky ball in her mouth:
She grips the ball, and put the other side in my hand;
To force me to play tug-of-war with her on demand:
Then, she finally released the ball
so that I can throw it across the room;
And she gallops after it, and returned it soon:
This, went on for a while, until I got hot and needed a fan;
The spoiled Shih Tzu went to sleep, because,
I was still rubbing him with my left hand:
The Pit finally got tired, and eventually, she fell asleep;
And, to my surprise, she released the ball from her teeth.

## World Pool of Fun...

She's in the whirlpool, having lots of fun,
swirling around, and around;
But, her feet are too short to touch the ground:
Wee! is the sound she makes, as she goes;
Faster, and faster, she can't go slow:
The fun, the fun, it never ends;
You better keep it going, if you want to be her friend:
The water's cold, but she doesn't mind;
She's having so much fun, she's just fine:
She's happy as can be;
Swirling around, and around, for all to see:
I'll take her picture, if I will;
She's moving too fast, she won't stay still:
She's on a floaty twirling fast;
She'll go on for hours, so the fun will last:
She's clapping, and laughing out loud;
When you see her, she'll make you smile,
It really is a sight to see;
Cause, she's happy as can be:
She doesn't want this fun to stop;
Cause, if it does, she's going to 'pout':
But, I got to let her know real soon;
That, it's time to get out of this 'whirlpool'!

## Entertain...

I'll do-what-I-do, to please the crowd;
I use my mic, to speak out loud:
And, when I'm done, I'll take a bow;
Cause, I know I've made my mother proud:
I'll show the world what God has given;
How he's blessed me, while I'm living:
How rich my life has become;
Because I'm filled-up with Jesus' love:
I'll help you all to understand;
How, I praise 'Our Father' on demand:
I came out to entertain you;
And, make sure you're blessed when I'm through:
I have all God's treasure stored inside;
My cup runneth over, before your eyes:
I want the whole world to know what God has done;
How, he blessed me, through his only son:
Yeah, I came out to entertain you;
And, I hope your soul is saved when I'm through:
I want you all to hear me clear;
Jesus is healing when Our father is here:
All of us must cry out loud;
And, he'll bless each one of us in the crowd:
I just stopped by to tell you a story;
How, all of us can give God the glory!
Just, bless his name, when we pray;

# LET IT OVERFLOW

And, he'll stay with us, throughout our day;
No weapon formed against us will do us harm;
While we have Jesus in our heart, we're in his arms:
Let's call his name as we lift our hands;
And he'll bless us with his perfect plan:
Now, in this room God's grace remains;
And I pray you've all, been entertained.

# All Your Kisses...

I want one of your kisses;
That I been missing:
Kiss me twice;
Cause I'm nice:
Okay, now three;
Kisses for me;
I got four;
But, I need some more:
I want five;
Cause I'm alive:
Give me six;
Oh, how I wish:
I want seven
All the way to heaven:
Give me eight;
Don't be late;
Give me nine:
That's just fine:
I want ten;
Now, let's do it again!

## Slumlord...

It's frustrating when you work real hard;
And you come home to broken appliances
because you have a slumlord:
Your fridge went out, and foods all spoiled;
And your stove won't heat so the water won't boil:
Your heat doesn't work when it's cold outside;
And when it's hot, your air won't blow, and you're about to die;
Your ceiling is leaking from a messed-up roof;
And your windows are rattling cause they're not weatherproof;
Your electricity when out in half of the house;
But, when the bill came, you still paid the full cost:
The banister's crooked, and the stairs are steep;
You fell off the porch, and didn't recover for a week:
There's fallen branches from a dead tree covering the backyard:
You try to clean them up, and you work real hard:
There is mold and mildew in your tub;
And it's always there, even after you scrub:
The plasters pilling from several different walls:
And there are huge rat holes, up and down the hall:
The rooms are small and without any closets;
So, you hang your clothes anywhere, it-allows-it:
Your carpet is musty, old, and dry-rotten:
It's been down for years, and it's just been forgotten:
Your basement flooded, and the floors never dry;
And, your pipes are leaking, and your water bill's high:

So, you call your landlord, but they don't answer their phone;
And they try to pretend as if they're not at home:
But, they get your money, and spend it quick;
But they don't fix a thing after you paid your rent:
Now, your backs up against the wall,
and you have nowhere else to go;
Cause, you're old and tired, and it's starting to show:
You want to tough it out, and you try your best;
But you're frustrated, and fed up with the mess:
Now, they're trying to sell their ragged-old house;
But, everyone refuses to pay their jacked-up cost:
Now, you're on your knees praying real hard;
Because you're still stuck with these same old 'Slumlords.'

## The Birthday Dinner...

I went out to dinner, for a birthday party;
It was 10 of us all together, and we ate very hearty:
It was an Italian restaurant with red, and white wine on the venue;
With a little bit of Italy on the menu:
Each of us ordered something different
that we couldn't pronounce;
And, we got a belly full of laughs trying to say it out loud;
I ordered a chicken breast that
I'd never had prepared that way before;
After taking the first bite, I wanted more:
It was a boneless filet, with a hard-textured crust;
And it was so tasty; I couldn't get enough:
It had a splash of lemon, with an after-buttery taste;
It was yellowish, and kind of clumpy, like a paste:
Whatever the name was, it tasted pretty-good to me;
It was served with spinach leaves,
and potato wedges covered with parmesan cheese:
Then I said to my mama "all this is, is just some sauté chicken,
with some lemon sauce";
And she looked at me and said:
"girl I'll don't believe you let that come out your mouth"!
My sons were there, as well and they had a ball;
One of them sent his food back, talking about,
he doesn't eat onions at all:
In Italy, they use onions, for one of their main ingredients;

And, they're always used, in every one of their seasonings:
Everybody thought for sure; he'll have an allergic reaction;
So, he ordered something without onions, to his satisfaction:
But, the chef made him a dish without any sauce;
It was so dry; it stuck to the roof of his mouth:
He drank two glasses of soda, just to wash it down;
And, the expression on his face, was not a smile:
We were all feeling good, and taking lots of pictures;
The room was filled with so much laughter; no one was listening:
We were laughing out loud, and acting real bold;
Our ethnicity is Africa American descendants,
and we're full of soul:
Now, the birthday boy was on the other side of the room;
He was sitting with his fiancé, looking real cool:
This extravaganza was planned by his fiancé;
She got us all together, and he wouldn't have had it any other way;
Next to his fiancé, was his son, alone with his wife;
They both came out to share the fun for the night:
To her left was her father and her aunt;
They came so we'll all know, what family love, is all about:
Our server was impressed to see all the love in the room;
He took a group picture, and said "please come back soon":
We all came together, in a special way;
To celebrate my brother-in-law's 65th birthday!

## If You...

If you gargle when you goggle, that makes you goofy;
If you squirt when you slurp, that makes you silly;
If you dazzle when you dance, that makes you dopey;
If you party when you play, that makes you preppy;
If you wobble when you walk, that makes you wacky;
If you calm when you cry, that makes you crafty;
If you ran when you run, that makes you ready;
If you whine when you read, that makes you weird;
If you anxious when you eat, that makes you extra;
If you praise when you pray, that makes you worthy;
If you fumble when you fight, that makes you funny;
If you laugh when you listen, that makes you looney;
If you tick when you talk, that makes you tender;
If you stumble when you stand, that makes you stable;
If you sign when you study, that makes you smart;
If you learn when you lay, that makes you lonely;
If you keep what you kept, that makes you kind;
If you jam when you jolly, that makes you jealous;
If you right when you wrong, that makes you-you!

## JACQUELINE JAMES

## Don't Wash my Dishes...

My biggest wishes;
Are don't wash my dishes:
When you wash them, you make a mess;
Then I'm left to clean up the rest:

You leave them filled with grease and grime;
And it's like that, every single time:
It's-as-if, you never use the soap at all;
And, you splatter water all over my wall:

I refuse to eat again from that plate;
I see the leftover food, from yesterday, I just ate:
And the glasses are fuzzy; they're not clear;
There's grime all over them, and dirt that's smeared:

The forks and spoons have food caked-on;
You could've scrubbed it off; it wasn't hard:
Now, let's talk about the pots and pans;
You left so much bacteria on them;
I can't touch them with my hands:

You call this clean? Get on out of my kitchen!
Can you hear? Are you listening?
Now, that's not right-you know is wrong;
Stop washing my dishes, why aren't you gone!

# Let It Overflow

You're not doing me no favor;
By, giving me some extra labor:
You leave stuck on food, that makes it harsh;
That I have to go back, to clean, and wash:
You're not helping me, that's a fact;
Just rinse and stack, now remember that!

# Chapter 6

## Special Dedication

1. My Angel
2. For Your Health
3. My First
4. My 'Sister'
5. Sister in Christ

## My Angel...

Oh, my little angel, as precious as can be;
It was my granddaughter, looking up at me:
As I touched her tiny hands, and her little bitty feet;
She began to cry, cause it was time to eat:
So, I warmed up her bottle, and fed her in my arms;
Then at an instance, she turned on her charm:
All my love came fluttering through;
This darling was mine, and she was so cute:
For I saw an angel, wrap in a blanket;
And looked up to God, and I just had to thank him:
As wonderful as the moment was, it couldn't last forever;
Cause, she had to grow up and become a lot better:

Dedicated to: My Beautiful Granddaughter Angel J. Griffin

## For Your Health...

You must be devoted, study hard, and learn a valuable lesson;
And be fully committed to work in the healthcare profession:
There are two types of people who work in this field;
For some it's their 'passion,' for as-long-as they live:
Others choose it for a job;
And, are only there for a while:
There's some who takes care of you;
And the others who care for you:
The ones who take care of you;
Only does what the chart, instructs them to do:
However, the ones who 'care' for you, while taking care of you;
Go above and beyond to see your recovery through:
As a physician, they must be exceptionally gifted to comprehend;
The complexity of a human body and within:
Their careers go much further than their paycheck;
Their ambition project to surpass the best:
It's a blessing to get one who cares for you;
They'll go the extra mile to consult with you:
Whether your prognosis is serious or not;
They research diligently for a diagnosis, and never stop:
I was assigned a doctor to follow my care;
She scrutinized my condition, making sure it's not severe:

*Continued On Next Page*

# LET IT OVERFLOW

She makes a difference in my doctor visit;
She prescribes the necessary medications, not the ones prohibited:
I glad to have met her acquaintance;
Through her services my health care isn't tainted:
I know that she won't be my doctor for long;
After she graduates, she must move on:
However, while I'm under her care, I'll utilize her expertise;
Because with her services I'm very pleased:
We were brought together, through her profession;
We formed a rapport, that'll keep us connected:
May she exceed highly on all her endeavors;
And the 'passion' she has will last forever:

Dedicated to: Dr.Joyce Ji

## My First...

You're an awesome daughter, and a wonderful 'Mother';
I wouldn't trade you for the world; I wouldn't want any other:
I'm glad you're mama's first-born child;
Cause I could love you for a longer while:
I had you when I was so very young;
We grew up together and had lots of fun:
I enjoyed the days I spent with you;
I keep them as precious memories - And I hope you do too:
Even though a lot of your time was spent with my mother;
She was trying to make up for losing her daughter:
Eventually, you got other sisters and brothers;
But, you're very special because you were
the first born to your mother:
Now you're an adult with a daughter of your own;
I still see you as my baby, even though you're grown:
Now you're going to understand some of the challenges
I had to go through;
And it's all so worth it, to see 'mother and daughter,'
love growing true:
I love you my beautiful baby girl;
And you're extra special cause you're my first
I brought into this world:

Dedicated to:
Sherece Gecelle Whitehorn

## My "Sister"...

One of the saints in our church sings, and shouts
like no tomorrow;
For all her joys, and her sorrows:
It's truly remarkable the way she praises;
Giving God the glory for her days:
She'll have the children sing for hours;
She's in charge of our youth choir:
They faithfully follow her instructions;
Pleasing the Lord with their selections:
Through their melodies, we're all uplifted;
She's very humble and exceptionally gifted:
The beauty she brings radiates throughout the room;
Her praises reassure us, our blessings are coming soon:
She spends a lot of time after work;
Cause she's heavenly involved in the church:
She has a family of her own;
And she taught all her children to sing gospel songs:
It's truly a blessing when she's near;
You'll always feel how much she cares:
She's an incredible 'sister' through Christ!
May God continues to bless her throughout her life:

Dedicated to: Sister Bell

## Sister in Christ...

It's a very special saint in the house;
She expresses the Holy Ghost through her mouth;
When she sings with praise, I always rejoice;
My heart is filled with her heavenly voice:
Throughout the church, we're all inspired;
It's an honor to have her in our choir:
She lifts our spirit with her song;
The melody stays in my head all day long:
I know she's a very faithful Christian;
So, when she speaks, I stay to listen:
I want to get to know her better as a person;
It'll be a blessing, and that's for certain:
When she's near, she's filled with charm;
And I thank God for giving me her poem:
I pray that she's filled up, with Jesus' learning;
Because God is about to take her on an amazing journey:
There are some things about her that you need to know;
That God has blessed her from her head- to-her-toe:
I'm truly grateful that she's my sister through Christ;
And may God continue to bless her throughout her life:

Dedicated to: Sister Campbell